SPENCER

Boston's Beloved Marathon Dog

Barbara A. Walsh

Illustrations by
SHELBY J. CROUSE

Irish Rover Press

For Spencer

and

all dogs who light up the world with love.

SPENCER

They called him the angel dog.

Spencer had golden-colored fur, big brown eyes,
and a heart as big as the Boston skyline.
Wherever he went, he made people happy.

"You're like a little angel," his dad said. "You're too
good not to share."

Before he grew old, people all over the world would
know Spencer's name and how he cheered for thousands
of runners in a famous race called the Boston Marathon.

Spencer was no ordinary pup.

He learned new tricks quickly and posed for pictures like a movie star.

Like other golden retrievers, Spencer loved to carry things.

He clutched his favorite frisbee during walks, fetched letters and packages from the mail truck, and brought his own umbrella and floppy hat to the beach.

Spencer had a special gift and could sense if someone was scared, sad or lonely. His brown eyes studied their faces, and he'd offer his paw to say hello.

"Everything is going to be OK," he seemed to say.

Spencer's dad knew his dog could do more than make strangers smile.

"A lot of people in hospitals and nursing homes could use some extra love. Would you like to help them, buddy?"

Spencer wagged his tail.

If Spencer was going to be a therapy dog that comforted people, he had to work hard.

He trained for many hours, and learned to sit, stay, and come. He learned how to wave goodbye and stay calm in crowds or strange places.

His first job was at a school. The children were excited to meet him. They clapped their hands and waved hello.

Spencer turned to his dad, nervous. "It's OK," his father said.

Slowly, Spencer walked toward the students. They petted his furry head and told him, "We love you."

He rested a paw in their laps, as if to say, "I love you, too."

Spencer and his family lived in Massachusetts, where the Boston Marathon began over 100 years ago.

Every April on Patriots Day, 30,000 runners came from all over the world to race 26 miles along hilly roads and steep streets.

Huge crowds cheered for the athletes. They hooted, hollered, and clanged cowbells.

The race was like a giant celebration.

But one year, in 2013, two men set off bombs that hurt hundreds of people, and some of them died.

Everyone was scared and sad. Suddenly, a happy race ended with many tears.

The next year, runners and fans returned to the Boston Marathon, but many people were worried that something bad might happen again.

Spencer's family knew their angel dog could help them be brave.

They bought Spencer two flags. One had a red heart; the other said "Boston Strong."

Lots of people waved the Boston Strong banners to show they were proud of their city and the famous race.

As thousands of runners passed by, Spencer sat on the side of the road holding his flags. Athletes stopped to hug Spencer. Some cried happy tears, thankful for the dog who made them smile.

"Will Spencer be here next year?" athletes asked.

"Of course," his dad replied.

And so, the tradition began. Year after year, Spencer sat at Mile 3 of the Boston Marathon race route, cheering runners and reminding them that they were Boston Strong.

It was always a little cold during the marathon. But one April, the wind howled, and rain pelted the streets.

Spencer's dad wasn't sure his dog could sit in the cold rain for hours to root for the runners.

"What do you think, buddy?"

Spencer wagged his tail.

Dressed in his dad's raincoat, Spencer sat on a wooden box and held his Boston Strong flags. Shivering and cold, runners stopped to hug Spencer. The dog gave them hope and strength to finish the race.

Spencer's father took a video that day and shared it online. Thousands of people watched it, and soon Spencer's wet furry face flashed on television news shows across the country.

Athletes from all over the world began writing to Spencer.

"The marathon is so hard and so hilly," one lady said. "When I feel like giving up, when I feel like I can't run another step, I think of the angel dog holding his flags.

"And then I know I can make it to the finish line."

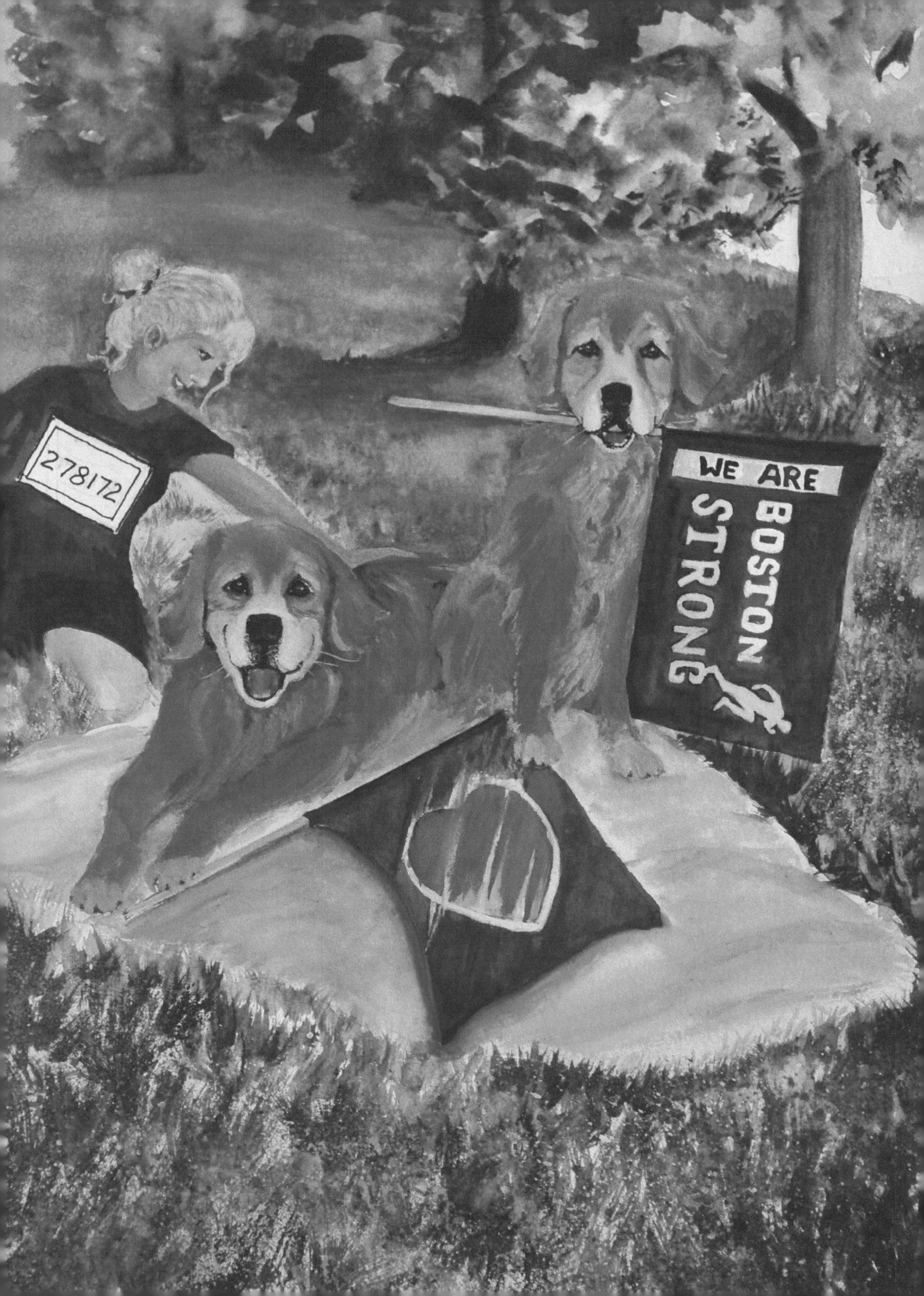
278172
WE ARE
BOSTON
STRONG

Although he had thousands of admirers, Spencer's number one fan was Penny, another golden-colored dog that his parents had adopted years earlier.

Spencer and Penny swam in the ocean together, chased each other in the backyard, and slept side by side.

But one day, Spencer didn't want to play. He lay on the floor and tried to tell his parents, "Something's wrong."

The veterinarian said Spencer was sick and had a bad lump in his body. The doctor removed it, and Spencer came home wagging his tail.

A year later, the veterinarian found another tumor. She gave Spencer medicine to feel better, and when the Boston Marathon began again, Spencer was ready.

The runners knew Spencer had been sick. They hugged him and knelt beside him for photographs.

"Keep fighting, Spencer!" they shouted.

When Spencer took a break, Penny picked up his flags, so her friend could rest.

A few days before the 2022 marathon, the people in charge of the race held a special celebration to honor Spencer. For eight years, he had cheered for runners in the rain, the cold and even when he was sick.

Like rock stars on their way to a concert, Spencer and Penny rode in a limousine to a fancy Boston hotel. A crowd of TV reporters waited and shouted Spencer's name as he leaped onto the red carpet.

During the ceremony, a roomful of people cheered as Spencer received his own race bib and was declared the official race dog of the 126th Boston Marathon.

Sitting tall and proud, Spencer flashed a toothy smile and beamed for the television cameras.

That summer, Spencer's family planned a birthday party for their angel dog.

Spencer was 13 now.

Seven hundred people – kids, dogs, and Boston Marathon runners – gathered to celebrate. Some people traveled from across the country.

They sang "Happy Birthday" to Spencer and to Penny, too. They gave them dog treats and toys that squeaked, and everyone, even the furry guests, ate lots of cake.

A few months before Christmas, Spencer stopped eating. He looked his dad in the eyes again, as if to tell him, "I don't feel good."

The doctor said Spencer had another tumor, and there wasn't anything they could do.

But Spencer didn't act sick. He still went on walks clutching his favorite frisbee. He fetched letters from the mail truck and visited nursing homes and schools to make people smile.

Not long after Valentine's Day, Spencer lay down on the living room floor. He began breathing hard and fast, like he had just finished his own marathon.

Spencer's mom and dad knelt beside him. They kissed his head and softly stroked his fur. Penny nuzzled her nose against her good friend's face.

"We will always love you," his dad whispered.

Spencer wagged his tail and closed his eyes.

People all over the world were sad that Spencer died.
They would miss the Boston Marathon's special fan.
On the day before that year's race, more than 200 golden-
colored dogs walked the last mile of the marathon to show
their love for Spencer and for Penny, who died soon after her
beloved friend.

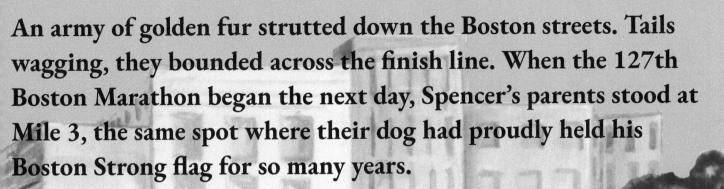

An army of golden fur strutted down the Boston streets. Tails wagging, they bounded across the finish line. When the 127th Boston Marathon began the next day, Spencer's parents stood at Mile 3, the same spot where their dog had proudly held his Boston Strong flag for so many years.

Runners shouted Spencer's name.

"We will never forget him," they promised.

Some runners said they felt Spencer's spirit and believed the angel dog was still watching over them, still cheering them on.

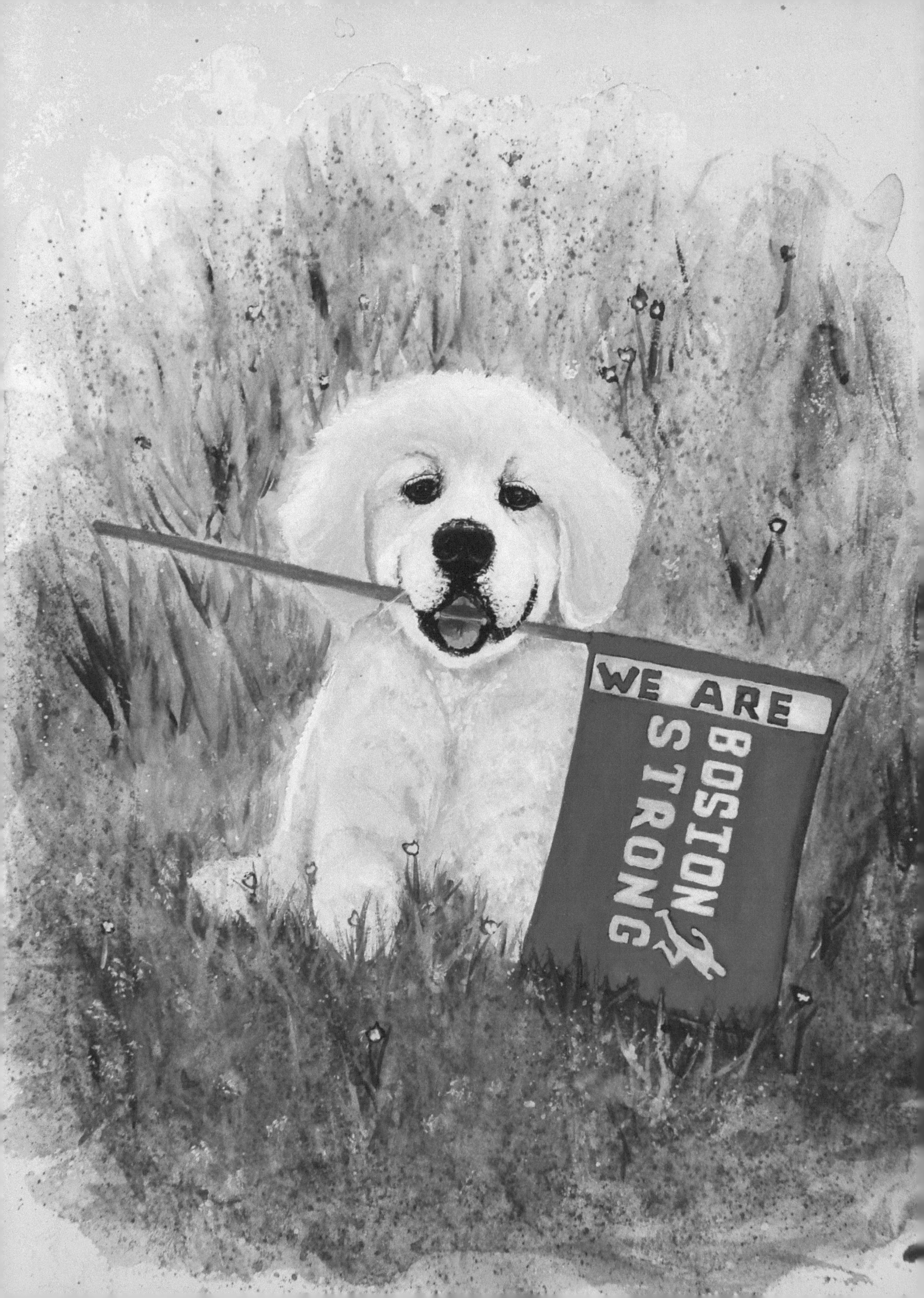
WE ARE
BOSTON
STRONG

As the spring flowers began to bloom, Spencer's family welcomed a new puppy into their home.

They named the dog Jimmy, and before long, the pup with the fluffy white-colored fur was posing for pictures and making friends with everyone he met.

Spencer's family missed their angel dog, and they missed Penny, too. They knew no other dog would ever take their place.

But maybe when Jimmy grew bigger, he could hold a Boston Strong flag and cheer for runners in the famous Boston race.

Maybe Jimmy could make lots of people happy and inspire them to never give up, to never lose hope.

Just like Spencer.

Soon after they adopted Spencer, Rich and Dorrey Powers knew they were blessed with a special gift, a dog that was too good not to share.

Fond of golden retrievers, they had welcomed several of the endearing and loyal dogs into their home. Penny, Spencer's beloved friend, was always by his side.

Both Spencer and Penny were trained as therapy dogs that comforted children and adults. Spencer gained worldwide fame as the beloved Boston Marathon dog who cheered for runners at Mile 3, the beginning of the 26.2-mile race route.

The Powers were devastated after losing both Spencer and Penny – who died of cancer within a week of each other in February 2023.

People around the world offered condolences and Massachusetts Golden Meetups, a group dedicated to golden retriever gatherings, organized a tribute. The day before the 2023 Boston Marathon, more than 200 dogs walked the last mile of the race to honor Spencer and Penny.

In memory of the cherished canines, the Powers and several groups donated nearly $40,000 towards dog cancer research at the Morris Animal Foundation. Fundraising has also begun to create a statue of Spencer holding his Boston Strong flags. The statue will be placed in Ashland, Mass., near the spot where Spencer cheered marathon runners for eight years.

Months after Spencer's death, Golden Opportunities for Independence, an organization that trains service dogs, donated a puppy to the Powers family. They named the fluffy white dog Jimmy, and he has begun therapy dog training so he can console school children and people in hospitals and nursing homes.

FMI on Spencer, Penny, and Jimmy: Spencer & Penny's Goldens Forever
https://www.facebook.com/Spencerpowrs

FMI on the Spencer statue:
https://www.gofundme.com/f/statue-of-spencer-boston-marathonofficial-dog

Barbara A. Walsh is a Pulitzer Prize-winning journalist and the author of six books, including *August Gale: A Father and Daughter's Journey into the Storm*, *The Lobster Lady: Maine's 102-Year-Old Legend*, and *Sammy in the Sky*, which is illustrated by artist Jamie Wyeth.

Barbara often writes about extraordinary Maine people and their pets. Dogs, especially rescues, have always graced her family's home.

Paco, the newest family member, is a "Sato," a street dog from Puerto Rico. An affectionate hound who has perfected the side eye, Paco has proven that if you rescue a dog once, it will rescue you a thousand times.

It was an honor, Barbara said, to write about Spencer, an extraordinary dog who inspired the world with his love. Barbara lives by the sea in southern Maine with her husband Eric and family.
FMI: barbarawalsh.net or bwalshauthor@gmail.com

Shelby J. Crouse grew up in western Maine, where beautiful landscapes and nature sparked her interest in art. Her journey as a self-taught artist unlocked unique techniques that contributed to her success. Shelby chose to work with watercolors, which reflect her free spirit.

Her family is fond of golden retrievers and has adopted four of them. Their newest dog, Brandi, embodies all the characteristics of a golden. She is loving and loyal, cherishing every moment spent by her family's side.

It was a privilege, Shelby said, to paint the illustrations for Spencer's story and capture his indomitable spirit with her art. Shelby has also painted drawings for two other books: *The Lobster Lady: Maine's 102-year-old Legend* and *The Adventures of Charlie: The Curious Cat and Me*. She lives in Brunswick with her husband Steve and family.
FMI: shelbycrouse@gmail.com

Irish Rover Press

Spencer: Boston's Beloved Marathon Dog

Copyright © 2023 Barbara A. Walsh

Paperback ISBN: 978-1-7374813-4-8

Hardcover ISBN: 978-1-7374813-5-5

Illustrations by Shelby J. Crouse

Photographs of Spencer and Jimmy by Rich Powers, owner of The Henry Studio.

Photograph of the Powers family and their dogs by Judy Ann Tucker.

Book Design by Clif Graves of HinterlandsPress.com